First World War
and Army of Occupation
War Diary
France, Belgium and Germany

60 DIVISION
181 Infantry Brigade
London Regiment
2/23 Battalion
15 June 1916 - 30 November 1916

WO95/3032/7

The Naval & Military Press Ltd
www.nmarchive.com
Published in association with The National Archives

Published by

The Naval & Military Press Ltd

Unit 10 Ridgewood Industrial Park,

Uckfield, East Sussex,

TN22 5QE England

Tel: +44 (0) 1825 749494

www.naval-military-press.com

www.nmarchive.com

This diary has been reprinted in facsimile from the original. Any imperfections are inevitably reproduced and the quality may fall short of modern type and cartographic standards.

© **Crown Copyright**

Images reproduced by permission of The National Archives, London, England, 2015.

Contents

Document type	Place/Title	Date From	Date To
Heading	WO95/3032/7		
Heading	60th Division 181st Infy Bde 2-23rd Bn London Regt Jun-Nov 1916		
Heading	War Diary of 2/23 Batt. London Regt From 15th June 1916 To 30th June 1916 Volume 1		
War Diary	Sutton Veny	15/06/1916	25/06/1916
War Diary	Havre	26/06/1916	26/06/1916
War Diary	En Route	27/06/1916	27/06/1916
War Diary	Villers Brulin	28/06/1916	30/06/1916
Heading	War Diary 2/23 Batt Lond Regt Volume 1 No.2 July 1-31 1916		
War Diary	France Villers Brulin	01/07/1916	06/07/1916
War Diary	Louez	07/07/1916	07/07/1916
War Diary	Trenches Abri Mouton	08/07/1916	15/07/1916
War Diary	Ecurie	16/07/1916	17/07/1916
War Diary	Trenches Ecurie	18/07/1916	20/07/1916
War Diary	Sabriere	21/07/1916	22/07/1916
War Diary	Trenches Sabriere	23/07/1916	27/07/1916
War Diary	Trenches	28/07/1916	28/07/1916
War Diary	Etrun	29/07/1916	31/07/1916
Heading	War Diary 2/23 Batt Lond Regt Volume I No.3 Augst 1-31.1916		
War Diary	Etrun	01/08/1916	05/08/1916
War Diary	Trenches	06/08/1916	13/08/1916
War Diary	Reserve Trenches Ecurie	14/08/1916	21/08/1916
War Diary	Trenches	22/08/1916	29/08/1916
War Diary	Etrun	30/08/1916	31/08/1916
Heading	War Diary 2/23 Batt. London Regt Volume I No.4 Sept 1-30 1916		
Miscellaneous	Appendix 1	01/09/1916	01/09/1916
War Diary	Etrun	01/09/1916	04/09/1916
War Diary	Firing Line	05/09/1916	10/09/1916
War Diary	Reserves	11/09/1916	16/09/1916
War Diary	Firing Line	16/09/1916	22/09/1916
War Diary	Reserve	23/09/1916	28/09/1916
War Diary	Firing Line	29/09/1916	30/09/1916
Heading	2/23 London Regt. War Diary From 1st October 1916 To 31st October 1916 Vol I No. 5		
War Diary	Firing Line	01/10/1916	04/10/1916
War Diary	Reserve	05/10/1916	10/10/1916
War Diary	Firing Line	11/10/1916	16/10/1916
War Diary	Reserve	17/10/1916	31/10/1916
Miscellaneous	Battalion Relief Orders By Lieut Col. H. Streatfeild Cmdg. 2/23rd Battn. The London Regiment	03/10/1916	03/10/1916
Miscellaneous	Battalion Relief Orders By Lieut Col. H. Streatfeild Cmdg. 2/23rd Battn. The London Regiment	09/10/1916	09/10/1916
Operation(al) Order(s)	2/23rd Battn. The London Regt. Order No.1	14/10/1916	14/10/1916
Miscellaneous	Report Of Raid Made By The 2/23rd Battalion The London Regt On Night Of 14/15th October 1916 In Enemy's Lines	15/10/1916	15/10/1916

Heading	War Diary 2/23 London R For November 1916 Vol 6		
War Diary	Candas	01/11/1916	04/11/1916
War Diary	Ergnies	05/11/1916	23/11/1916
War Diary	En Route for Marseilles	24/11/1916	30/11/1916

WO 95/3032/7

60TH DIVISION
181ST INFY BDE

2-23RD BN LONDON REGT

JUN - NOV 1916

TO SALONIKA
AND

TO FRANCE 1918 JUNE
30 DIV 21 BDE

181/60

WAR DIARY

of

2/23. Batt. London Regt.

From 15th June 1916 to 30th June 1916.

Volume 1

No. 1

Army Form C. 2118

WAR DIARY
or
INTELLIGENCE SUMMARY 2/23 Battalion, The London Regt

(Erase heading not required.)

Instructions regarding War Diaries and Intelligence Summaries are contained in F. S. Regs., Part II. and the Staff Manual respectively. Title Pages will be prepared in manuscript.

Place	Date	Hour	Summary of Events and Information	Remarks and references to Appendices
SUTTON VENY	15/6/16		Received Embarkation Orders for Overseas. Weather "Fine".	W/ST
"	16/6/16		Brigade Route March BOREHAM – SACK-HILL – POINT 690 BOVIS-BARROW – EAST-HILL CAMP HEYTESBURY – BRIGADE CAMP. Weather "Fine".	W/ST
"	17/6/16		"Fine". General Training.	W/ST
"	18/6/16		" A Interior Economy – Draft of men received recently from 3/9th Lond. Regt. commenced G.M.C.	W/ST
"	19/6/16		" Church Parade	W/ST
"	20/6/16		DULL & COLD. Brigade Route March HEYTESBURY – TYTHERINGTON – SUTTON VENY	W/ST
"	21/6/16		Fine. Getting in practise trenches, inspections &c	W/ST
"	22/6/16		Fine. Do.	W/ST
"	23/6/16		Fine. Do.	W/ST

1875 W¹. W593/826 1,000,000 4/15 J.B.C. & A. A.D.S.S./Forms/C. 2118.

Army Form C. 2118

WAR DIARY
or
INTELLIGENCE SUMMARY 2/23rd Batt. The London Regt
(Erase heading not required.)

Instructions regarding War Diaries and Intelligence Summaries are contained in F.S. Regs., Part II. and the Staff Manual respectively. Title Pages will be prepared in manuscript.

Place	Date	Hour	Summary of Events and Information	Remarks and references to Appendices
SUTTON VENY	24/6/16		Weather "Showery" Preparations to move	WRT
"	25/6/16		1st one Battalion left Sutton Veny Camp. 1st Train left Warminster 10-45 A.M. 2nd Train 11-55 A.M. — arrived Southampton 1-30 P.M. & 2-15 P.M. respectively. Transport loaded on S.S. Manchester Importer and Personnel on S.S. Connaught. Left Southampton 5-40 P.M.	WRT
HAVRE	26/6/16		Weather Wet Arrived 1 A.M. disembarked 7.20 A.M. and marched to Docks Rest Camp Left Rest Camp 6-5 P.M. and marched to Rly station, entrained & left 9.59 P.M. (Note 6 Officers & 120 Other ranks left at Rest Camp Passist Academy of Dist. Amm. Col)	WRT
EN ROUTE	27/6/16		Weather "Showery" En-route to Villers Brulin. Train stopped 3.45 A.M. Auffléa also at 10.35 A.M. at Abbeville 2 P.M. Battalion marches to Villers Brulin Train arrived Petit-Houvain Monterolier-Bucky, arriving 8/10 P.M.	WRT

1875 W: W.593/826 1,000,000 4/15 J.B.C. & A. A.D.S.S./Forms/C. 2118.

WAR DIARY
or
INTELLIGENCE SUMMARY

2/23 Batt. London Regt

Army Form C. 2118

(Erase heading not required.)

Instructions regarding War Diaries and Intelligence Summaries are contained in F. S. Regs., Part II. and the Staff Manual respectively. Title Pages will be prepared in manuscript.

Place	Date	Hour	Summary of Events and Information	Remarks and references to Appendices
VILLERS BROLIN	28/6/16		Weather Showery. Inspection & cleaning up of Billets. General kit economy Inspection. Party left at HAVRE 26/6/16 arrived 3-30 P.M.	W.O.T J.P.S
"	29/6/16		Fine. Short ROUTE MARCHES under Company arrangements	
"	30/6/16		Drizzle. Short ROUTE MARCHES under Coy. arrangements. Physical Training & Jim-Jaks. Lecture by Coy. Chemical Advisor 1 PM. 2nd Lt MACKAY, 3 N.C.O's v 9 men proceeded R.T.M School at N.R.S.F.	
			LIGNY ST. FLOCHEL	
			4 Officers, 8 N.C.O's & 4 Officers servants proceeded to Third Army School HERMAVILLE for course of instruction	

R.F. [signature]
Lieut Col
Comdg 2/23 London Regt

1875 W: W593/826 1,000,000 4/15 J.B.C. & A. A.D.S.S./Forms/C. 2118.

WAR DIARY
2/23. BATT LOND REGT
VOLUME I Nº 2
JULY 1-31. 1916

Army Form C. 2118

WAR DIARY
or
INTELLIGENCE SUMMARY
(Erase heading not required.)

2/23 Battalion, London Regt

Place	Date	Hour	Summary of Events and Information	Remarks and references to Appendices
France. Villers Brulin	JULY 1st	WEATHER. FINE.	Route marches, Physical Training, Instruction on Rapid wiring	W.D.1.
"	2nd	FINE.	Church Parade. Inspections & Interior Economy. Instruction on Rapid wiring.	W.D.1.
"	3	FINE.	Company Training and Gas Helmet practice, Rapid Wiring	W.D.1.
"	4	OVERCAST. Thunder Storm 2-5-30 PM	4 Platoons attended lecture at AGNIERES on Consolidation of craters. Rapid wiring. Bathing parades.	W.D.1.
"	5	DULL	Practice throwing of Live Bombs. Interior Economy &c.	W.D.1.
"	6	FINE. WET LATER.	6 AM Battalion moved by march route to forward area LOUEZ. Billeted for night in SUCERIE	W.D.1.
Louez	7	DULL. WET LATER.	Battalion moved into trenches by Platoons for instructional purposes under 154th Infantry Brigade.	W.D.1.
Trenches Abri Mouton	8	DULL FINE LATER.	Instructional work, 1 men wounded	W.D.1.
"	9	FINE	Instructional work, Lieuts Youne & Halcrow wounded. 2 men accidentally wounded. Church Parade for details at Louez	W.D.1.

Army Form C. 2118

WAR DIARY
or
INTELLIGENCE SUMMARY
(Erase heading not required.)

2/23 Batt. London Regt.

Place	Date	Hour	Summary of Events and Information	Remarks and references to Appendices
TRENCHES ABRI. MOUTON	JULY 10	WEATHER FINE.	Instructional work	
"	11	DULL.	Instructional work, one man killed, one man wounded (self inflicted) Capt Fox admitted hospital sick. Lt. Willson assumed duties of acting Adjt.	H.C.W.
"	12	DULL.	Instructional work.	H.C.W.
"	13	SHOWERY. FINE LATER.	Battalion took over section of trenches from 4th SEAFORTHS, starting midday	H.C.W.
"	14	WET. FINE LATER.	Situation normal, 5 men wounded, details moved to ETRUN from LOUEZ.	H.C.W.
"	15	FINE.	Situation normal, one man killed, 4 wounded, 4 Officers 2/Lieuts BARRETT, WOOD, HALL & MATTHEWS reported for duty	H.C.W.
ECURIE	16	FINE. WET LATER	Battalion moved to reserve trenches (being relieved by 2/21st LONd REGT.) one man wounded	H.C.W.
"	17	HEAVY RAIN DULL LATER	Situation normal	H.C.W.

Army Form C. 2118

WAR DIARY or INTELLIGENCE SUMMARY

2/23. Batt. The London Regt

(Erase heading not required.)

Instructions regarding War Diaries and Intelligence Summaries are contained in F.S. Regs., Part II. and the Staff Manual respectively. Title Pages will be prepared in manuscript.

Place	Date	Hour	Summary of Events and Information	Remarks and references to Appendices
TRENCHES	JULY.	WEATHER		
ECURIE	18	SHOWERY. DULL LATER.	Situation normal	K.G.W.
"	19	FINE	Situation normal, 1 man wounded.	K.S.W.
"	20	FINE	Battalion moved from reserve to front line trenches. Large damage done to parapet - fire steps by enemy's Genl. Mortars 1-30 p.m & 9 p.m Lewis Gun emplacement blown in, gun uninjured. Enemy's Observation Balloon destroyed 7.10 am. Damage to trenches repaired. One man wounded. Major Seyd admitted hospital sick. 2nd Lieut L.H. Reed reported for duty. Draft of 50 men of 3/10 London Regt. attached for duty.	K.C.S.
SABRIERE	21	FINE	Our Stokes Guns fired on enemy during afternoon, 2 Patrols each of 1 Officer & 2 men went out from 11 pm to midnight. enemy's wire penetrated doubtful if shelter front line held at all as 1 Officer went to junction of Sap 23c 98.96 nothing seen or heard. Enemy's snipers active. Trenches repaired & improved. Capt Fox returned to duty from hospital, 1 man wounded.	K.W.
"	22	FINE	Large amount of T.M. bombardment by enemy, our Artillery retaliated - our Lewis Guns disperses enemy working party 1 am Patrol went out 11 pm found very difficult to negotiate owing to Shell Holes - 2 men killed 6 men wounded	K.S.W.

Army Form C. 2118

WAR DIARY
or
INTELLIGENCE SUMMARY
(Erase heading not required.)

2/23 Batt. London Regt.

Place	Date	Hour	Summary of Events and Information	Remarks and references to Appendices
TRENCHES SABRIERE	JULY 23	WEATHER FINE.	T.M. Activity by enemy, our Artillery retaliated, Lewis Guns fired on enemy during night. 2 men wounded.	J.R.T.
"	24	FINE.	Bombardment of enemy lines by Trench Mortars. Enemy snipers very active, one observed fired on & dispersed. Trenches repaired & deep latrine constructed. 3 men wounded. 2nd Lieuts SWANSON, HALL & MATTHEWS proceeded on courses	J.R.T.
"	25	FINE.	Our wire examined 11/30 P.M. found weak in places. Lewis Guns fired at enemy working party with good results. Artillery fired on enemy, they retaliated with 50 77mm shells. — Hostile aeroplanes passed over front-line. 1 man killed.	J.R.T.
"	26	DULL	3 Patrols went out during night. Found enemy's wire very thick in good condition, patrols fired on but no casualties occurred. Enemy quiet. Major SEYD discharged from Hospital returned to duty.	J.R.T.
"	27	FINE	Situation normal, artillery active. 2nd Lieuts SWANSON & MATTHEWS returned from courses.	J.R.T.

Army Form C. 2118

WAR DIARY
or
INTELLIGENCE SUMMARY   2/23. Batt. London Regt.
(Erase heading not required.)

Place	Date	Hour	Summary of Events and Information	Remarks and references to Appendices
		WEATHER		
TRENCHES	JULY 28	FINE.	Situation normal, Battalion moved from front line trenches to rest Billets ETRUN (being relieved by 2/21st L. Regt	W.B.T. J.R.S.
ETRUN	29	FINE.	Interior Economy, Bathing parades &c 2nd LIEUT HALL returned from Course	J.R.S.
"	30	FINE.	Church parade, 2nd Lieuts HHIDDINGTON, SAYERS & MABEY proceeded on courses	W.B.T. J.R.S.
"	31	FINE.	Short Route marches by Platoons, Physical Drill, Inspection of Arms & Equipment.	W.B.T. J.R.S.

H Humphrys Lieut Col
Commanding 2/23 London Regt.

WAR DIARY
2/23. BATT LOND REGT
VOLUME I. N° 3.
AUGST 1-31. 1916

Army Form C. 2118

WAR DIARY
or
INTELLIGENCE SUMMARY 2/23 Battalion London Regt.
August 1916.
(Erase heading not required.)

Instructions regarding War Diaries and Intelligence Summaries are contained in F. S. Regs., Part II. and the Staff Manual respectively. Title Pages will be prepared in manuscript.

Place	Date	Hour	Summary of Events and Information	Remarks and references to Appendices
ETRUN	Augst 1st	Weather FINE	Route Marches by Companies. Physical Training &c. Signalling from Observation Balloon noticed at 9-45 P.M.	MBS
"	2nd	FINE	Bombs dropped from Hostile Aeroplane on station at 5/30 A.M, no damage reported. Route Marches, Physical Training. Bathing & Lieut F.A. Cooke returned today from Hospital.	MBS
"	3rd	FINE	Route Marches. Physical Training. Inspections &c Lieut G.H. BAKER & 2nd Lt. M.T. CHISHOLM proceeded on Anti Gas Course	MBS
"	4	FINE	Bathing. Physical Training &c	MBS
"	5	FINE	Battalion moved from Reserve Billets ETRUN to front line trenches SABRIERE. Capt. WILLS, 2nd Lieuts WHIDDINGTON & SAYERS held from Course, also Lts BAKER & CHISHOLM No Patrols sent out during night, our Artillery fired some shots on to THELUS about 7-30 P.M. At mid-night enemy opened heavy Artillery bombardment against Batt on our right. The rest of this bombardment just caught right of our line, no damage done, our Artillery replied	BS

1875 Wt. W593/826 1,000,000 4/15 J.B.C. & A. A.D.S.S./Forms/C. 2118.

Army Form C. 2118

WAR DIARY
or
INTELLIGENCE SUMMARY 2/23 Battalion London Regt.
(Erase heading not required.)

Instructions regarding War Diaries and Intelligence Summaries are contained in F.S. Regs., Part II. and the Staff Manual respectively. Title Pages will be prepared in manuscript.

August 1916.

Place	Date	Hour	Summary of Events and Information	Remarks and references to Appendices
TRENCHES	Aug 6	FINE	2/Lieut. H.D BAKER admitted to Hospital sick. 2/Lieut. L.H READ returned from course. No patrols went out during the night, at 10-30 PM our Artillery opened heavy bombardment on left, a certain amount of retaliation was received but no damage was done. Hostile aeroplanes passed over at about 5.30 PM was a result about 7.30 PM the enemy Howitzers branches ground between RIPPERT & SABRIERE about 14 - 5.9 Shells, at about 5 falling besides, one shell landed in SABRIERE Enemy fired between 12-15 rounds from large M.H. between 10-45 PM midnight - no damage being done.	W.R.T.
"	7	FINE	2/Lieuts. MOLLER, TURNER & DAVIS reported for duty. LIEUT FLINT J. wounded, 1 man KILLED, 3 men wounded during raid on enemy trenches. Raid was effected on enemy trenches @ 9-30 PM considerable information being gained — many casualties to enemy reported. At 12.40 PM we fired on enemy with 3" T.M's received a certain amount of retaliation from their T.M's field artillery. At 3.30 PM our heavy artillery fired about 30 rounds with good effect on enemy's front line E of LILLE ROAD	W.R.T. See Appendix 1.

Army Form C. 2118

WAR DIARY or INTELLIGENCE SUMMARY

(Erase heading not required.)

2/23 London Regiment.

Instructions regarding War Diaries and Intelligence Summaries are contained in F.S. Regs., Part II. and the Staff Manual respectively. Title Pages will be prepared in manuscript.

Place	Date	Hour	Summary of Events and Information	Remarks and references to Appendices
TRENCHES	Augst Walker		Capt TAYLOR proceeded on course.	
	8	FINE	1 man reported missing after raid of last night. At 3.47 PM our 3" TRENCH MORTARS bombarded the enemy front line for about 20 minutes. Working party reported by our patrols at 12.15 AM in their front line trench opposite S.AP.21. 15 rounds fired on them from "A" Battery in conjunction with fire from our Lewis guns. At 9-10 PM 3 of our aeroplanes flew over the enemy lines. An enemy aeroplane tried to cross our line at 12.45 PM but turned back on being fired on by our guns. Our trenches repaired where damaged by enemy T.M's.	WBT
	9	FINE	Very quiet day, at 9 PM our T.M's fired about 100 rounds into enemy trenches. The enemy sent over a few T.M's, rifle grenades about 12.30 PM falling chiefly into S.AP.21, our artillery retaliated at 1-2 PM.	WBT
	10	FINE	3 men KILLED & 6 men wounded. The morning was quiet, at about 6 PM our T.M's opened fire on enemy's front line doing considerable damage to parapet, consolidation fires from T.M's aerial torpedoes, again at 10-30 PM our T.M's opened fire on enemy. The enemy continued firing T.M's aerial torpedoes during night causing a certain number of casualties.	WBT

Army Form C. 2118

WAR DIARY
or
INTELLIGENCE SUMMARY
(Erase heading not required.)

2/23 London Regiment

Place	Date	Hour	Summary of Events and Information	Remarks and references to Appendices
TRENCHES	Augst 11	FINE Weather.	3 men KILLED & 3 men WOUNDED, Capt WILLS & 2nd Lieut MOLLER slightly wounded. Casualties occurred during bombardment. Started fast night continued till nearly dawn. At 8.30 PM our TM's bombarded enemys lines saw tracks of our Artillery, good results were observed on enemys front lines. Enemy replied. Our bombardment doing slight damage to our trenches. At 10.15 PM enemy MG opened fire for about 1 hour evidently reaching for our MG's no damage was done.	MBF
	12th	FINE	Morning quiet, enemy damage considerably about 2.30 PM. Cap. N° 22 with A.T's between 4 & 7 PM our Artillery TM's fired on enemy. Several shots falling in his front line. Several heavy shots were also fired into THIELOS. Enemy replied well. Our fire between 4 & 7 PM throwing over heavy TM's damaging CHEMIN CREUX & BONNAL completely filling fire bay in BONNAL L.25. Patrol of 2 Officers & 3 men went out at 11.30 PM. No enemy seen or heard. Trenches Repaired where damaged. One man wounded. 2nd Lieut MATTHEWS proceeded on course.	MBF

Army Form C. 2118

WAR DIARY
or
INTELLIGENCE SUMMARY 2/23 London Regiment.
(Erase heading not required.)

Instructions regarding War Diaries and Intelligence Summaries are contained in F.S. Regs., Part II. and the Staff Manual respectively. Title Pages will be prepared in manuscript.

Place	Date	Hour	Summary of Events and Information	Remarks and references to Appendices
	Augst	Weather		
TRENCHES	13	FINE	At 2 AM we again bombarded enemy's line, about 30 minutes later this was taken up by Artillery & TM's on our left, after sending up several Red & then Green rockets. The enemy retaliated but ceased as soon as we did about 2.50 AM. Battalion relieved by 2nd London Regt & moved themselves ECURIE. 1 man wounded.	WBT.
RESERVE TRENCHES ECURIE.	14	SHOWERY.	Situation normal. 2nd Lieut DAVIS proceeded on Bombing course.	WBT.
"	15	SHOWERY	Situation normal. Draft of 50 men arrived.	WBT.
"	16	FINE & Cloudy.	Situation normal.	WBT.
"	17	FINE Heavy Showers later	Situation normal	WBT.
"	18	FINE early Showers later	Situation normal. Capt S.C.W. OWEN admitted to Hospital sick. MAJOR H.E. PEMBERTON admitted Hospital for treatment having been bitten by cat.	WBT.

Army Form C. 2118

WAR DIARY
or
INTELLIGENCE SUMMARY 2/23. London Regiment.
(Erase heading not required.)

Instructions regarding War Diaries and Intelligence Summaries are contained in F.S. Regs., Part II. and the Staff Manual respectively. Title Pages will be prepared in manuscript.

Place	Date	Hour	Summary of Events and Information	Remarks and references to Appendices
	August	Weather		
RESERVE TRENCHES ECURIE	19th	Showery	Situation normal. 2nd Lieut R.R.WOOD admitted Hospital, sick.	M.T.
"	20	Showery	Situation normal. Capt OWEN reported duty on discharge from Hospital. 2nd Lieut L.H READ proceeded on course. 2 Lieut DAVIS returned from course. 2nd Lieut JONES reported for duty from base	M.T.
	21	FINE	2nd Lieut MATTHEWS returned from course. Battalion moved from reserve trenches to front line relieving 2/21st L Regt. One man wounded during relief. 3.15 P.M. our Artillery fired on enemy's front line. Enemy rather more active sent M.G fire at 11.30 P.M. BONVAL trench repaired up 20 deepened at different places.	M.T.

1875 Wt. W593/826 1,000,000 4/15 J.B.C. & A. A.D.S.S./Forms/C. 2118.

Army Form C. 2118

WAR DIARY
or
INTELLIGENCE SUMMARY   2/23 Battalion London Regt
(Erase heading not required.)

Instructions regarding War Diaries and Intelligence Summaries are contained in F.S. Regs., Part II. and the Staff Manual respectively. Title Pages will be prepared in manuscript.

Place	Date	Hour	Summary of Events and Information	Remarks and references to Appendices
TRENCHES	August 22	FINE	Enemy's front & support lines bombarded between 22.b.60.35 & 23.a.50.43 by 2" & 3" T.M's at 11a.m - 2.30.p.m - 7.45 P.M the enemy trenches being badly knocked about. The 11.A.M bombardment was deliberate & a certain amount of retaliation was received - the enemy replied to 2/30 bombardment doing considerable damage to BONVAL. They reply to 7.30 bombardment was very feeble. General trench repair, especially BONVAL. 1 man killed & one man wounded. J.B.T.	
	23	SHOWERY.	General bombardment Enemy's lines by 18.lb, 2" & 3" T.M's intermittently throughout the day doing a good deal of damage Enemy's front & support lines enemy's reply from bombardments was very weak. At 8/45 PM a heavy bombardment started on our right lasting about 2 hours. General service fairly active. 2nd Lt W.D. BAKER returned from Hospital J.B.T.	

1875. Wt. W593/826 1,000,000 4/15 J.B.C. & A. A.D.S.S./Forms/C. 2118.

Army Form C. 2118

WAR DIARY
or
INTELLIGENCE SUMMARY
(Erase heading not required.)

2/23. London Regt.

Instructions regarding War Diaries and Intelligence Summaries are contained in F.S. Regs, Part II. and the Staff Manual respectively. Title Pages will be prepared in manuscript.

Place	Date	Hour	Summary of Events and Information	Remarks and references to Appendices
TRENCHES	Augst 24	FINE Weather	Site intermittently bombarded the enemy's lines throughout the day - at 9 PM again at 11 PM Heavy fire was opened for short intervals. At 11 PM our Lewis Guns opened fire on enemy's working parties continuing for about 1 hour. Enemy's retaliation on the whole very weak. 1 man wounded.	JRJ
	25	FINE Showery later.	Lieut J FLINT awarded Military Cross. Intensive bombardments were carried out by our 3" T.M's, assisted by 2 2" T.M's and 18 pounders at 3-45 P.M., 6-30 P.M. & 7.15 P.M., considerable damage to enemy's trenches appears to have been done. An Indian patrol went out at 10.15 P.M. About mid-night a small German working party seen opposite Sap 23 & dispersed by Lewis gun fire. Enemy reply bombardments was weak little damage being done. Enemy aircraft was more active than usual especially between 10.45 A.M. & 2 P.M. 2 men wounded.	JRJ

Army Form C. 2118

WAR DIARY
or
INTELLIGENCE SUMMARY 2/23 Batt. London Regt
(Erase heading not required.)

Instructions regarding War Diaries and Intelligence Summaries are contained in F.S. Regs., Part II. and the Staff Manual respectively. Title Pages will be prepared in manuscript.

Place	Date	Hour	Summary of Events and Information	Remarks and references to Appendices
	August	Weather		
TRENCHES	26	Showery.	Artillery 2" & 3" T.M's fired intermittently during whole day, a few heavy shells were observed (blond) in THELUS & the MILL. At 2-30 P.M. about 30 rifle grenades were fired into enemy's front line. Enemy kept up steady fire of T.M's & A.T's during the afternoon & at 7.30 PM they fired about twenty rifle grenades at SAP.23. 2nd Lieut JONES proceeded on Anti Gas course. J.B.J	
"	27	Heavy rain early Fine intervals heavy showers later	We intermittently (contoraded) enemy bans during the day, very little retaliation being received. Suspected M.G emplacement in enemys front line bombarded wrecked. Indian Patrol went out at 11 P.M. 2nd Lieut READ returned from course. 2nd Lieut MOLLER proceeded on Bombing course. Lieut F.R. STONE & 12 O.Ranks reported for duty. 1 man wounded. J.B.J	

Army Form C. 2118

WAR DIARY
INTELLIGENCE SUMMARY
(Erase heading not required.)

2/23 Batt. London Regt.

Instructions regarding War Diaries and Intelligence Summaries are contained in F.S. Regs., Part II. and the Staff Manual respectively. Title Pages will be prepared in manuscript.

Place	Date	Hour	Summary of Events and Information	Remarks and references to Appendices
TRENCHES	Augt 28	Weather. Heavy showers. Fine intervals.	Enemy bombarded our lines with TM's at 11 AM. 2.30 PM & 6.30 PM considerable damage being done to BONNAL. 1 man killed & 3 wounded. Major SEYD admitted to Hospital, sick. 2/Lieut TURNER proceeded on P. training course.	JHBJ
	29	Still rain. Heavy T. storm 4.30 PM Gale & rain throughout night.	2.10 AM heavy bombardment lasting about 1 hour opened on enemy's lines. Battalion moved by platoons from front line to reserve billets ETRUN being relieved by 2/24 L. Regt. 2nd Lieut JONES returned from course.	JHBJ
ETRUN	30	GALE & heavy rain.	Bathing & Interior Economy. 1 man died as result of Self inflicted wound.	JHBJ
	31	FINE	Route marches, instructing in rapid wiring, bay. fighting, Bombing &c MAJOR SEYD returned today from hospital. Major McGALL DAA & QMG declared Officers @ 11 AM	JHBJ

[signature] Lieut Col.
Commanding 2/23 London Regt.

WAR DIARY

2/23 Batt. London Regt.

VOLUME I. No 4.

SEPT. 1-30. 1916.

Vol 4

APPENDIX 1.

Two parties under Lieut. J. Flint and 2nd Lieut J.L. Hunt respectively raided the enemy trenches on the night of the 7/8th about A.23.g.99.77. and A.23.d.10.67., the primary object being to obtain identification by taking a prisoner.

The party under Lieut. Flint entered the enemy trenches but were unable to secure identification. They, however, bombed severely several dugouts inflicting considerable casualties on the enemy.

Our casualties were: Lieut Flint severely wounded, one man missing, one killed and 13 other ranks wounded.

Lieut-Colonel.
Cmdg. 2/23rd Battn. The London Regiment.

1/9/16.

Army Form C. 2118

WAR DIARY
or
INTELLIGENCE SUMMARY

2/23 Batt. London Regt

(Erase heading not required.)

Instructions regarding War Diaries and Intelligence Summaries are contained in F. S. Regs., Part II. and the Staff Manual respectively. Title Pages will be prepared in manuscript.

Place	Date	Hour	Summary of Events and Information	Remarks and references to Appendices
ETRUN	Sept 1	Fine & Dull	Enemy dropped several shells into ETRUN between 1.15 & 1.45 P.M. Some casualties. 2nd Lieut W.T. CHISHOLM & 1 man died of wounds received. General training, rapid wiring, Gas helmet practice &c.	J.R.J.
"	2	Fine, some rain.	General training, wiring, Bombing &c. 2nd Lieut TURNER returned from course.	J.R.J.
"	3	Fine	Church Parade. Physical training, wiring, bathing. 2nd Lieut W.B. BAKER admitted Hospital sick.	J.B.J.
"	4	Wet morning. Fine later. Wet evening.	Battalion moved from Rest Billets & Firing line relieving 2/21st London Regt at 5.30 P.M. 6.30 P.M. & 7 P.M. our Stokes guns fired on enemys front line 7 P.M. enemy replied & did some damage (our right front) they also sent over a few phosphorous shells on RIGHT COLLECTOR, no damage done.	J.R.J.
FIRING LINE	5	Dull Rain later	Intermittent Bombardment throughout day by our T.M's, very little retaliation. 3 patrols went out during night to inspect enemys wire, new trench connecting up Bn. on right. Capt FOX admitted hospital sick, Capt TAYLOR ret'd from course.	J.W.

Army Form C. 2118

WAR DIARY
or
INTELLIGENCE SUMMARY 2/23 Batt. London Regt.
(Erase heading not required.)

Instructions regarding War Diaries and Intelligence Summaries are contained in F.S. Regs., Part II. and the Staff Manual respectively. Title Pages will be prepared in manuscript.

Place	Date	Hour	Summary of Events and Information	Remarks and references to Appendices
FIRING LINE	Sept. 6		Weather- Drizzle. Intermittent bombardment. Throughout day Barked enemy retaliated rather more than usual damages normal. Patrol went out during night & examined Crater on left. Found they were not occupied by enemy, another patrol was sent out & found that our wire was badly damaged between SAP. 21 & 22, this was at once repaired.	H.W.
"	7		Our 18 pounders, 2" & 3" T.M's & aft grenades were fairly active throughout the day bombarding enemys front support lines. Enemy was very active between 3-30 & 4.30 PM and again between 6, 8, 7 PM sending over a large number of T.M's falling mostly between BONNAL & COLLECTER trenches. Left of SP. Gun position (L.22.c.20) was smashed in. Patrols were sent out - found wire had been badly damaged in places repairs were carried out at once. Patrols also went out & examined enemys wire found same in good condition between 11 AM & 12.30 PM they were Enemy planes flew over our lines but did not return for some time. Shelled by our AA Guns. BONNAL repaired.	H.W.

Army Form C. 2118

WAR DIARY
or
INTELLIGENCE SUMMARY

2/23 Batt. London Regt.

(Erase heading not required.)

Instructions regarding War Diaries and Intelligence Summaries are contained in F.S. Regs., Part II. and the Staff Manual respectively. Title Pages will be prepared in manuscript.

Place	Date	Hour	Summary of Events and Information	Remarks and references to Appendices
FIRING LINE	Sept 8	Weather FINE	We bombarded the enemy's trenches at intervals throughout the day with 18 pounders 2" & 3" T.M's - rifle grenades were also fired. The enemy sent over a good number of A.T's (Whizz bangs - T.M's but on the whole was much quieter than usual. Several patrols went out during the night & found enemy's wire in good condition. Work repairing BONHIL continued. Lt HODGES proceeded to ETAPLES (sick) 2nd Lt MOLLER admitted to Hospital (Sick) 5 men wounded.	A.W.
"	9	FINE	Intermittent bombardments throughout the day, enemy working parties seen by patrols directly N. of Sap.23 was dispersed by Lewis Gun fire. Enemy replied with our bombardments from 1PM to 6PM. He sent over a large number of Oil Cans, all of them were air burst & exploded over CHEMIN CREUX at 6PM 2 heavy shells exploded on the BIDOT near new T.M emplacement. Entrances to SAPS 23-24 & 26 repaired. Lieut HOLMES returned from course. 2nd Lieut W.D. BAKER evacuated sick to England & struck off strength. 3 men wounded.	A.W.

Army Form C. 2118

WAR DIARY
or
INTELLIGENCE SUMMARY 2/23 Batt. London Regt.
(Erase heading not required.)

Instructions regarding War Diaries and Intelligence Summaries are contained in F.S. Regs., Part II. and the Staff Manual respectively. Title Pages will be prepared in manuscript.

Place	Date	Hour	Summary of Events and Information	Remarks and references to Appendices
FIRING LINE	Sept. 10	FINE but DULL	Weather. Battalion moved from Firing line to Reserve trenches ECURIE being relieved by 2/21st Batt. London Regt. Situation Normal.	H.W.
RESERVES	11th	FINE some rain later	Situation Normal. 2 Lt MATTHEWS admitted to hospital, sick.	H.W.
	12	DULL to SHOWERY	Situation Normal. 2nd Lt ALLEN admitted to Hospital, sick.	H.W.
	13	SHOWERY	Situation Normal. 2 Lt SEABROOK A.L. reported for duty with battalion. 2 Lt SWANSON proceeded to Base Depot for duty.	H.W.
	14	SHOWERY	Situation Normal. ECURIE defences were manned. Lieut MABEY proceeded on leave from course.	H.W.
	15	FINE	Situation Normal. Capt FOX returned to duty from Hospital.	H.W.

Army Form C. 2118

WAR DIARY
or
INTELLIGENCE SUMMARY

2/23 Batt London Regt.

(Erase heading not required.)

Instructions regarding War Diaries and Intelligence Summaries are contained in F.S. Regs., Part II. and the Staff Manual respectively. Title Pages will be prepared in manuscript.

Place	Date	Hour	Summary of Events and Information	Remarks and references to Appendices
RESERVES to FIRING LINE	Sept. 16	FINE	Situation Normal. Battalion moved from reserve trenches to firing line. Our Field Artillery and 2" T.M's were cutting wire on enemy front line at intervals during the day. At noon our 18 pounders put a few shells in THELUS. Enemy was fairly active during the day, considerable damage was done to BONNAL especially in L.25 where a heavy T.M. bomb landed on the trench completely destroying a fire bay making a crater about 14ft in diameter. Work on repairing damage commenced.	JFW
	17th	FINE	Our Artillery, T.M's, Stokes guns were again very active throughout the day. Considerable damage appears to have been done to enemy wire, a number of shells were put into THELUS. Enemy was active during the day with light artillery, T.M's & A.T's. Besides a few rifle grenades BONNAL was damaged at L.23, L.24 & L.25, 2 men being killed & burried at L.25 by heavy T.M. considerable damage was also done in SAP 26. Enemy also bombarded BIDOT from BONNAL to ABRI CENTRAL, no damage was done BONNAL repaired & other damage made good. SAP 22 could not be repaired owing to enemy's rifle grenades & A.T's. Capt. UNDERWOOD proceeded on course at AUXI LE CHATEAU	JFW

Army Form C. 2118

WAR DIARY
or
INTELLIGENCE SUMMARY 2/23 Batt. London Regt.
(Erase heading not required.)

Instructions regarding War Diaries and Intelligence Summaries are contained in F. S. Regs., Part II. and the Staff Manual respectively. Title Pages will be prepared in manuscript.

Place	Date	Hour	Summary of Events and Information	Remarks and references to Appendices
FIRING LINE	Sept 18	Weather WET	Our Artillery was quite active throughout the day shelling the enemys front & support lines & putting a few shells into THELUS. Our T.M's again cut enemys wire, observation was difficult owing to rain & mist. Enemy was active with T.M's & A.T's also rifle grenades, right BONNAL was damaged in several places. Trenches are in a very bad state owing to heavy rain. BONNAL was almost impassable in several places on account of parapet & parados caving in. Repairs to trenches carried out. 10 men reported for duty.	JCW
	19	SHOWERY	Our Artillery, T.M's & Stokes guns were very active on enemy's front line during the day. Our heavier guns bombarded THELUS, Lewis guns dispersed enemy working party opposite L.21 @ 10 P.M. Enemy was very active doing considerable damage to BONNAL, a number of direct hits were secured & 1 man was killed at junction of S.21 & BONNAL. The greatest damage was done on the left–with heavy A.T's. Officers patrols report that enemys wire has been badly smashed but not demolished. All available men repaired damage to BONNAL &c	JCW

1875 Wt. W593/826 1,000,000 4/15 J.B.C. & A. A.D.S.S./Forms/C. 2118.

Army Form C. 2118

WAR DIARY
or
INTELLIGENCE SUMMARY

2/23 Batt. The London Reg.

(Erase heading not required.)

Instructions regarding War Diaries and Intelligence Summaries are contained in F.S. Regs., Part II. and the Staff Manual respectively. Title Pages will be prepared in manuscript.

Place	Date	Hour	Summary of Events and Information	Remarks and references to Appendices
FIRING LINE	Sept 20	Weather SHOWERY	Our Night Artillery shelled enemy front & support lines & TMEWs intermittently during the day, our T.M's also destroyed enemys wire. Enemy was more quiet than usual during the day, a few T.M's, A.T. & rifle grenades were fired, Also 8 of the T.M's overnight direct hits in BONNAL. Patrol went out during night reported enemys wire strong in places. Trenches are in a very bad state owing to enemys shelling & heavy rain, BONNAL is in an especially bad condition being impassable at several points. Our men are working on repairs night & day.	
"	21	Overcast	Air were fairly active during the day with 4·5, 18prs TMs & Stokes guns on enemys front & support lines. Our T.M's badly damaged enemys wire & we scored a number of direct hits on his trenches. Enemy shelled BONNAL intermittently throughout the day but no damage was done — on the whole he was more quiet than usual, enemy had working parties out near — A. 22. b 5·3 @ 2/30 these were fired on & dispersed by our Lewis guns. Patrol went out from L.20 g. P.M. & 11·30 P.M. are from L.21 — 12pm–4/30 AM & 1pm–4/30 AM. reported enemys quiet. Trenches still in very bad state, all available men repairing same.	

1875 Wt. W593/826 1,000,000 4/15 J.B.C. & A. A.D.S.S./Forms/C. 2118.

Army Form C. 2118

WAR DIARY
or
INTELLIGENCE SUMMARY   2/3 Batt. London Regt.
(Erase heading not required.)

Instructions regarding War Diaries and Intelligence Summaries are contained in F.S. Regs., Part II. and the Staff Manual respectively. Title Pages will be prepared in manuscript.

Place	Date	Hour	Summary of Events and Information	Remarks and references to Appendices
	Sept.	Weather		
FIRING LINE	22	FINE	Battalion moved from firing line to Divisional Reserve ETRUN being relieved by 2/21st Batt. London Regt. 1 man Killed & 4 wounded.	
RESERVE	23	FINE	Interior Economy, Baths & General cleaning up. Lt. MABEY returned from course.	
"	24	FINE	Church Parade. Fatigues. Intensive Digging &c. Capt. Owen admitted Hospital. Sick.	
"	25	FINE	Fatigues. Intensive digging. Revetting. General training.	
"	26	FINE	Fatigues. Intensive digging. Representative party marched to ECOIVRES on occasion of L/Cpl BRADLEY being presented with D.C.M. by Corps Commander. 2nd Lieuts SCOTT & ANDREWS reported for duty with Battalion.	
"	27	FINE	Battalion inspected @ 11.45am by Corps Commander Lt. Gen. Sir C. FERGUSON Bt. KCB, MO, DSO. Bathing & General Fatigues. 2/Lt HALL admitted hospital, sick. 2/Lt FORD reported for duty.	

Army Form C. 2118

WAR DIARY
or
INTELLIGENCE SUMMARY

2/23 Batt. London Regt.

(Erase heading not required.)

Instructions regarding War Diaries and Intelligence Summaries are contained in F. S. Regs., Part II. and the Staff Manual respectively. Title Pages will be prepared in manuscript.

Place	Date	Hour	Summary of Events and Information	Remarks and references to Appendices
RESERVE	Sept 28	FINE & Weather FINE to DRIZZLE	Battalion moved from Divisional Reserve to FIRING LINE relieving 2/21 Batt London Regt.	WDF
FIRING LINE	29	FINE	Our TMs, Stokes guns & Rifle grenades fired intermittently throughout day on enemys front & support lines, patrols went out & examined wire & found it weak in places. Enemy put a few TMs & light shells into BONNYK & BIDOT damaging latter in two places. But on the whole day was quiet. Trenches are still in bad state but all available men are repairing same.	WDF
	30	FINE	On the whole day was fairly quiet, our bombarded enemys front & support lines, they retaliated with a few TMs & examined enemys wire &c. Patrols went out & examined enemys wire &c.	WDF

W. Greenfield
Lieut Col.
Commanding 2/23 London Regt.

SECRET.

Vol 5

2/23 LONDON REGT.

WAR   DIARY.

From 1st October, 1916.

To 31st October, 1916.

VOL. I. No. 5.

-----------oOo-----------

Army Form C. 2118

WAR DIARY
INTELLIGENCE SUMMARY
2/23 Batt. London Regt

(Erase heading not required.)

Instructions regarding War Diaries and Intelligence Summaries are contained in F.S. Regs., Part II. and the Staff Manual respectively. Title Pages will be prepared in manuscript.

Place	Date	Hour	Summary of Events and Information	Remarks and references to Appendices
FIRING LINE	OCTOBER 1st	Weather FINE	Officer Patrols went out at 1-20 A.M. & 3-30 A.M. returning at 5 A.M. They reported that enemy's wire did not appear to be seriously damaged in places by our recent Stokes Gun bombardments. Enemy were heard working hard on repairing his front line but none of enemy were seen. Our Artillery was fairly active during day shelling on enemy front & support lines & THELUS. Our T.M's & S.Guns fired intermittently during day. Enemy sent over a few A.T.s, T.M, & Light Shells, none of which did any damage. On the whole the day was quiet. Enemy is apparently very short of ammunition. Between 5-40 & 6 P.M. two of our aeroplanes were dropping red, white & green lights, one flame being over THELUS, the other opposite ARRAS. Enemy working party was seen at A.22.b.7.6 @ 11 A.M. they were wearing green tunics & round green caps with a white band. This party was pointed out to F.O.O. who ordered a few shells to be sent over which apparently did no damage as party was seen again shortly afterwards. They were fired on by our snipers but were out of range of rifles. At 9.15 P.M. several Germans were seen on their front line. They were fired on by our Lewis Guns. Enemy has strengthened wire by throwing spools over his parapet, a great number of flares are still sent up. 8 General repairs to trenches carried out, new latrine dug in L.24. One man wounded, shell shock.	

Army Form C. 2118

WAR DIARY
or
INTELLIGENCE SUMMARY   2/23 Batt London Regt
(Erase heading not required.)

Place	Date	Hour	Summary of Events and Information	Remarks and references to Appendices
FIRING LINE	October 2nd	Weather WET	Our Artillery, T.M's & Stokes Guns fired intermittently during the day, we also sent over a number of rifle grenades. An enemy working party was seen at A.22.b.9.4 @ 11/15 AM this party was fired on & dispersed by our 8 pounders, another party seen at noon was dispersed by Lewis Guns. An Officer patrol left Sap 20 @ 10/20 PM returning at 11/15 PM patrolling was very difficult owing to stat-I found & extreme darkness, they report enemy heard working on his 2nd line. Except for a very few shells A.T's & rifle grenades enemy was very quiet all day. He appears to be working hard on his support lines. Green parachute lights seen on his right at 8.30 & 9.20 PM at 11.10 PM enemy sent up a red rocket, no result, observation very difficult owing to mist. 2 enemy aeroplanes were seen flying very low flying over their own trenches opposite our left front @ 8/30 AM. Enemy still appears to be working very hard on his support lines & to be neglecting his front lines at most points. Our trenches are again getting into a bad state owing to wet weather, all available men are at work revetting & repairing same. 2nd Lt. S.L.T. P.G. reported for duty.	

1875 Wt. W593/526 1,000,000 4/15 J.B.C. & A. A.D.S.S./Forms/C. 2118.

Army Form C. 2118

WAR DIARY
or
INTELLIGENCE SUMMARY   2/23 London Regt
(Erase heading not required.)

Instructions regarding War Diaries and Intelligence Summaries are contained in F.S. Regs., Part II. and the Staff Manual respectively. Title Pages will be prepared in manuscript.

Place	Date	Hour	Summary of Events and Information	Remarks and references to Appendices
FIRING LINE	OCTOBER 3rd	Weather WET	There was the usual Artillery, T.M. & Stokes Gun activity during the day firing on enemy front & second line trenches, many RIFLE GRENADES were also sent over. About 3.15 P.M. our Heavy Artillery fired on enemy position in rear of NINE ELMS, some shells were seen to burst N of THELUS. The enemy has been rather more active during the last 24 hours sending over several WHIZZ BANGS, about a dozen T.M's were also sent over (the greater portion of which did not explode. During the afternoon the enemy sent a few 5.9 shells over to the rear. Rifle Grenades were fired into the BONVAL but little damage was done. Smoke was seen rising from enemy front line towards LILLE ROAD & at 4/15 P.M. large columns of smoke were seen to rise from centre of THELUS. It drove two enemy aeroplanes flying South over our own lines dropped a RED, 2 WHITES & a GREEN LIGHT, no result. The work of stumping & relaying floor boards along whole of BONVAL continued, BONVAL revetted where fallen in.	

Army Form C. 2118

WAR DIARY
or
INTELLIGENCE SUMMARY

2/23 Batt, London Reg.

(Erase heading not required.)

Instructions regarding War Diaries and Intelligence Summaries are contained in F. S. Regs., Part II. and the Staff Manual respectively. Title Pages will be prepared in manuscript.

Place	Date	Hour	Summary of Events and Information	Remarks and references to Appendices
	October	Weather		
FIRING LINE	4	WET, some FINE INTERVALS	An Officer Patrol went out at 4/15 A.M. (to examine enemy's wire), the party was fired on by a sentry of the Battalion on our right (H.L.I.) one Officer (Lt. B.H. Mc.BIRNEY) was badly wounded, 2/Lt HUNT was wounded by barbed wire but remained at duty. The morning was fairly quiet & the Battalion was relieved by 2/21st Batt. London Regt. moved to Reserve trenches, ECURIE. 2nd Lieut. G.F. HENDY reported for duty.	Appendix 1. JM B.T. JM B.T.
RESERVE	5	DULL to FINE	Situation Normal, general repair to trenches carried out, particular attention being paid to sumping.	JM B.T.
"	6th	FINE, WINDY	Situation normal, repairs to trenches proceeded with. Lt. G.H. BAKER returned from course. 2nd Lt. HALL returned to duty from Hospital.	JM B.T.
	7th	SHOWERY & WINDY	Situation Normal.	JM B.T.

WAR DIARY
or
INTELLIGENCE SUMMARY

Army Form C. 2118

2/23 Batt. The London Regt.

(Erase heading not required.)

Place	Date	Hour	Summary of Events and Information	Remarks and references to Appendices
RESERVE	October 8	Met. early FINE later	Situation normal. The general condition of the trenches has suffered from the adverse weather conditions, all available men employed in company repairing same. A raid was carried out at 6-5 P.M by 2/22 London Regt resulting in 4 prisoners being captured. Gas was discharged by Batt on right, during which time Gas Helmets were worn.	Appendix I
"	9	DULL	Situation Normal. The defences of ECURIE manned for practice purposes during evening.	Appendix I
"	10	FINE	Battalion moved from reserve to FIRING LINE relieving the 2/21 London Regt no casualties occurred during relief. The enemy was fairly active with T.M's particularly on our left, some damage was done to BOHNAL between S.24 & S.26. At 3 P.M three of the enemy were seen behind wrecked aeroplane, in a trench. They were fired on & disappeared. BOHNAL repaired where damaged & general repairs carried out.	Appendix II

Army Form C. 2118

WAR DIARY
or
INTELLIGENCE SUMMARY 2/23 London Regt.
(Erase heading not required.)

Instructions regarding War Diaries and Intelligence Summaries are contained in F. S. Regs., Part II. and the Staff Manual respectively. Title Pages will be prepared in manuscript.

Place	Date	Hour	Summary of Events and Information	Remarks and references to Appendices
FIRING LINE	October 11th	Weather. SHOWERY. WINDY	About 11-30AM our T.M's & Stokes Guns retaliated to enemy's T.M's & effectively silenced them. our T.M's continued to bombard enemy front line till about 12-30 PM. At 2 P.M. we bombarded enemy wire opposite S.21 & made a breach through it. From 3. PM till about 4/30 PM we bombarded enemy's front & 2nd lines with T.M's & Stokes Guns. From 11 A.M to 1 PM the enemy the enemy bombarded our front line with T.M's left of S.24, considerable damage was done to BONNAL. From 2-30 to 4-20 PM enemy's Sap bombarded BONNAL with A.T's & RIFLE GRENADES but no damage was done by these. A man's head was visible above the enemy 2nd line trench behind wrecked aeroplane. he was wearing a light blue pill-box cap & several times during the day he was seen & men entering a dug out in enemy front line. Damage done to BONNAL was repaired, fire from S.21 to night repaired & strengthened. 1 man killed & 2 wounded during the day. Lt Col H.S STREATFEILD proceeded on leave & MAJOR V. SEYD assumed temporary command.	

V.S.

Army Form C. 2118

WAR DIARY
or
INTELLIGENCE SUMMARY 2/23 London Regt.
(Erase heading not required.)

Instructions regarding War Diaries and Intelligence Summaries are contained in F. S. Regs., Part II. and the Staff Manual respectively. Title Pages will be prepared in manuscript.

Place	Date	Hour	Summary of Events and Information	Remarks and references to Appendices
FIRING LINE	OCTOBER 12th	DULL Weather	An Officer Patrol went out at 12.30 AM between SAPS 23 & 24, nothing was encountered & they had nothing to report, another Officers Patrol went out at 2 AM from SAP 21 & also with nothing to report — From about 11.30 AM to 2.30 PM our heavy Artillery bombarded the hay-stacks right of the BOIS CARRE, & from 2/15 PM to 2/45 PM our artillery bombarded enemy front & second lines on our right & also 2" T.M's cut the enemys wire opposite SAPS 21 & 23. From 3 to 4/30 PM our STOKES Guns fired on enemys front line opposite SAP 20, RIFLE GRENADES were fired intermittently throughout the day. Throughout the day the enemy was very active with T.M's & Aerial Torpedos, during the afternoon he hit & damaged one of our STOKES Guns @ the L.20 emplacement. Throughout the night the enemy bombarded our Sap heads with rifle grenades. One green light was seen on our right @ 10/50 PM, no result. BONHAI repaired & revetted, entrance to SAP 21 repaired & general repairs to trenches proceeded with.	

J.W.S.C.

1875 Wt. W593/826 1,000,000 4/15 J.B.C. & A. A.D.S.S./Forms/C. 2118.

Army Form C. 2118

WAR DIARY
or
INTELLIGENCE SUMMARY   2/23 LONDON REGT.
(Erase heading not required.)

Instructions regarding War Diaries and Intelligence Summaries are contained in F.S. Regs., Part II. and the Staff Manual respectively. Title Pages will be prepared in manuscript.

Place	Date	Hour	Summary of Events and Information	Remarks and references to Appendices
FIRING LINE	OCTOBER 13th SUCHEZ	Dies Non	At 6.30 AM BIDOT was blown in where it joins BOHNAL. Our Artillery showed very little activity during the day, at 2/15 PM we sent over a few 18 pounders, a few Zerschek appeared to be duds. Our 2" T.Ms bombarded enemy front line & wire throughout the day & at 10 PM our Stokes Guns bombarded enemy front line on our left. The enemy was extremely active with rifle grenades throughout the day, on our left enemy T.Ms were active, a large proportion exploding on our wire. At 12/45 PM a large enemy Howitzer flew in the entrance to the mine shaft near our left front Coy HQrs. Between 3-30 & 4/30 pm a number of small T.Ms were sent over our left front a large proportion of which did not explode. At 10-50 PM a party of the enemy was seen approaching our line on the left, they were driven off with rifle fire, at the same time 6 or 8 ATs fell in the vicinity of left Coy HQrs. About noon 2 or 3 shells from enfiladed left COLLECTOR one exploding near LILLE ROAD. Four Officer Patrols inspected our wire between SAPS 23 & 26. reported some badly damaged several unexploded T.Ms were found amongst our wire. During our Stokes Gun bombardment enemy sent up StarShells Rockets at intervals of 2 mins. More was no result. At 8 PM 2 of our Aeroplanes flew over enemy lines & were fires on by H.Guns. Damage to trenches repaired.	[signature]

WAR DIARY or INTELLIGENCE SUMMARY 2/23 London Regt.

Army Form C. 2118

Place	Date	Hour	Summary of Events and Information	Remarks and references to Appendices
FIRING LINE	October 14	Dull Weather	Our Artillery was very in-active throughout the day, at 2/30 to 2/45 PM we sent a few 18 pounders on to enemy's 2nd line & our T.M's bombarded enemy's front line & wire opposite SAPS 21 & 23. At 11 PM our STOKES Guns bombarded enemy front line opposite SAP 21 preparatory braid sending over in all about 600 shells at the same time we sent over a few 18 pounders. About 10.15 AM enemy started bombard with T.M's, A.T's & Rifle grenades, particularly the foot, the flew in BOHHAT in 5 places. At 3 PM enemy sent over a number of Whizz bangs most of them falling on left front. In reply about 11 PM bombardment enemy sent over many Oil cans & rifle grenades from duck COLLECTEUR was continually enfiladed by M.G fire. The enemy parapet came to be badly damaged along most of our front, & particularly opposite SAP. 23. At about 6/30 PM what appeared to be a big fire was observed in direction of ARRAS. At the commencement of our bombardment enemy sent up red rockets later single green rockets were sent up, result was the cessation of firing by their Artillery on right, & to shorten the range of their Artillery on left. Work of repairing trenches &c continued. Capt UNDERWOOD returned from course	N87

1875/Wt. W593/826 1,000,000 4/15 J.B.C. & A. A.D.S.S./Forms/C. 2118.

Army Form C. 2118

WAR DIARY or INTELLIGENCE SUMMARY

2/23 London Regt.

(Erase heading not required.)

Instructions regarding War Diaries and Intelligence Summaries are contained in F.S. Regs., Part II. and the Staff Manual respectively. Title Pages will be prepared in manuscript.

Place	Date	Hour	Summary of Events and Information	Remarks and references to Appendices
	OCTOBER	Weather		
FIRING LINE	15	DRIZZLE	At 3 AM raid was carried out on enemy trenches (see Appendix attached)	Appendix III
		FINE LATER	our Heavy Artillery, S Guns & T.M.s cooperated. bombarded enemy trenches	
		Heavy rain every afternoon	on left. In reply our bombardment enemy sent over a great many rifle grenades, M.T.s & T.M.s	
			Our Howitzers bombarded enemy lines & supposed T M emplacements from 11·15 to 11·50 AM.	
			He sent over 18 pounders intermittently throughout the afternoon.	
			At 10·20 enemy sent over a few rifle grenades which burst in BOHAIN at rear of A.G.	
			From 11 AM to dusk enemy bombarded intermittently with T M's. 6 heavy T M's landed in	
			S.24. but failed to explode, three were found N° 10 "Shells	
			Between 9 & 10 P.M. enemy sent over many Del Carro which burst near LILLE ROAD, this	
			was in retaliation to bombardment (by Brigade on our left).	
			Dummy bombardment on our left enemy sent up Zared lights & 18 green, about same	
			time 3 bright green lights were seen on our extreme right.	
			At 9·15 PM two red rockets were sent up opposite S.24.	
			Lapham party was seen on the right about 12·30 PM they were scattered by	W.B.F.
			our Lewis Gun fire.	
			Repairs to trenches proceeded with.	
	2	11.00 a	proceeded on Lewis Course. J. HOLMES proceeded on Inf training course.	

1875 Wt. W593/826 1,000,000 4/15 J.B.C. & A. A.D.S.S/Forms/C. 2118.

Army Form C. 2118

WAR DIARY
or
INTELLIGENCE SUMMARY 2/23 Batt. London Regt.

(Erase heading not required.)

Instructions regarding War Diaries and Intelligence Summaries are contained in F.S. Regs., Part II. and the Staff Manual respectively. Title Pages will be prepared in manuscript.

Place	Date	Hour	Summary of Events and Information	Remarks and references to Appendices
	OCTOBER	Weather		
FIRING LINE	16	FINE	Throughout the day Heavy Artillery in conjunction with T.M's bombarded suspected T.M. position, considerable damage appeared to be done.	JHBT
		RAIN LATER	The enemy did not reply to Bombardment but a few Rifle Grenades were sent over during the evening.	
			Aircraft were very active all day & enemy aircraft was very active during the evening.	
			Battalion was relieved by 2/21 Batt. London Reg. — during evening & completed by 1.30 AM 17/10/16.	
RESERVE	17	FINE to SHOWERY	Interior Economy, Bathing &c. 2Lt FORD returned from course	JHBT
	18	DRIZZLE Some fine Intervals	Route Marching, Intensive digging, Bayonet fighting &c 2/Lt STREATFEILD returned Rally from Leave. Lt BAKER proceeded on course (*SHIPING*)	JHBT
	19	VERY WET	Interior Economy, Inspections &c 2nd Lt R.R. HOOD returned from Course Lt HODGES returned to duty from Hospital	JHBT

Army Form C. 2118

WAR DIARY
or
INTELLIGENCE SUMMARY
2/23 Batt. The London Reg.
(Erase heading not required.)

Place	Date	Hour	Summary of Events and Information	Remarks and references to Appendices
	October	Weather		
RESERVE	20	FINE	Short Route Marches by Coys. Intensive Digging, Bayonet fighting &c. Gas demonstration roll call. Coys dismiss afternoon. 2nd Lt R.R. Hood admitted Hospital, sick.	J.B.7.
"	21	FINE	Short Route Marches by Coys. Intensive Digging, Bayonet fighting &c.	J.B.7.
"	22	FINE	Church Parade, Bathing & General cleaning up preparatory to moving.	J.B.7.
"	23.	DULL	Battalion moved by march route from ETRUN to IZEL LES HAMEAU en-route for GHQ reserve and billeted there for the night.	J.B.7
"	24	WET	Battalion proceeded en-route to TIERNEY	J.B.7. J.B.7.
"	25	SHOWERY	Re-distribution of Billets, Interior Economy &c.	J.B.7.
"	26	FINE to SHOWERY	Route marching, Physical training &c.	J.B.7.

WAR DIARY
or
INTELLIGENCE SUMMARY

(Erase heading not required.)

Army Form C. 2118

2/23 Batt. London Regt

Place	Date	Hour	Summary of Events and Information	Remarks and references to Appendices
RESERVE	OCTOBER 27	SHOWERY	Route Marching, Physical Training &c. Capt H.B.Fox (Adjutant) admitted Hospital, sick. Lt Oppenheimer ad Hospital, sick. Capt A.H.Crabbe appointed Acting Adjutant.	a.s.c
	28	DULL	Battalion moved (by march route) from IVERGNY to BARLEY. & billetted for the night	a.s.c
	29	WET & COLD	Battalion moved by march route from BARLEY to OUTREBOIS & billetted	a.s.c
	30	SHOWERY & COLD	Battalion moved by march route from OUTREBOIS to CANDAS & billetted	a.s.c
	31	SHOWERY	Morning parade. Physical Training, practice in the attack by Platoons &c.	a.s.c

W Crowfoot
Lieut Col
Comdg 2/23 London Regt

BATTALION RELIEF ORDERS
by
Lieut-Col. H. Streatfeild
Cmdg. 2/23rd Battn. The London Regiment.

APPENDIX. 1

In the Trenches.   3/10/26.

---

1. The Battalion will be relieved to-morrow the 4th inst., by the 2/21st Battn. The London Regt. and will proceed to "C" Position to relieve the 2/22nd Battalion, The London Regiment.

2. Companies will be relieved as follows:-

   "A" Company will be relieved by "D" Coy. 2/21st commencing about 2.30 p.m. and will proceed to ABRI MOUTON via FANTOME Trench.
   "B" Company will be relieved by "C" Coy. 2/21st commencing about 2 p.m. and will proceed to SUNKEN ROAD via BLANCHARD, ROCLINCOURT AVENUE and HIGH STREET.
   "C" Company will be relieved by "A" Coy. 2/21st commencing about 2.50 p.m. and will proceed to ABRI CENTRAL.
   "D" Company will be relieved by "B" Coy. 2/21st commencing about 3.10 p.m. and will proceed to ECURIE via CHEMIN CREUX, BLANCHARD, ROCLINCOURT AVEUE, VILLAGE STREET.
   Signallers will be relieved by 11.30 a.m.
   Bombers will be relieved by 12 p.m. and will proceed to ABRI MOUNTON.
   Snipers will be relieved by 11 a.m. and will proceed to ABRI CENTRAL.

3. One Officer and One N.C.O. from each Company will be sent in good time so as to arrive at new position 1½ hours in advance.

4. O.C. Companies will personally report relief complete at SABLIERS on the way down and will hand in the usual certificates and will report by Runner to "C" Position when they have relieved the 2/22nd Battalion.

Capt. & Adjt.
2/23rd Battn. The London Regiment.

BATTALION RELIEF ORDERS.
by
Lieut Col. H. Streatfeild
Cmdg. 2/23rd Battn The London Regiment.

APPENDIX II

October 9th 1916.

The Battalion will be relieved tomorrow in "C" position, and will move to "A" position to relieve the 2/21st Battalion The London Regiment.

Dispositions of Companies in Right 1 will be as follows:-

"D" Company.............Right Front
"C" Company.............Left Front
"A" Company ....Right Support
"B" Company.............Left Support.

One Officer and one N.C.O. per Company will be sent to Right 1 about 1½ hours before relief tomorrow to take over Trench Stores.

"B" Company will leave their present position at 10 a.m.
"C" Company will leave their present position at 10.30 a.m.
"D" Company will, on relief, immediately move to the right front.
"A" Company will leave their present position at 12.30 p.m.

Bombers, Machine Gunners and Snipers will complete their relief by 10.30 a.m.

All Signallers, except two per station, will be in their new positions in Right 1 by 10.30 a.m.

"A", "B" and "C" Companies will leave 1 Officer and 1 N.C.O. behind to hand over Trench stores to the incoming Companies of the 2/21st Battalion.

The whole relief must be complete by 3.30 p.m.

The completion of the relief will be reported by runner to Battalion Headquarters,

The attention of Company Commanders is called to Battalion Order dated 8/10/16, para 2, re Company Gas N.C.Os' duties.

Captain & Adjutant
2/23rd Battalion The London Regiment

9/10/16

SECRET.

APPENDIX III

2/23rd Battn. The London Regt.

Order No. 1.

Reference = $\frac{1}{10,000}$ Roclincourt and Trench Maps.

1. A raid on the German Trenches at point A.23.e.98.87 will be carried out by a party of the 2/23rd Battn. The London Regt.

2. OBJECTS.
   (i) To obtain indentification.
   (ii) To cause all possible damage.

3. ZERO. Time and date to be notified later.

4. RAIDING PARTY. as under:-
   O.C. Lieut. G.H. Baker.

   Right Blocking Party...1 N.C.O. & 5 men) under 2/Lt.
   Right Raiding Party....1 N.C.O. & 7 men) H.E. DAVIS.

   Left Blocking Party....1 N.C.O. & 5 men) under Lieut.
   Left Raiding Party.....1 N.C.O. & 7 men) G.H. BAKER.

   Blanket men & Orderlies 1 N.C.O. & 4 men) under 2/Lt.
   Rear Party..............2 N.C.O. & 10 men) A.L. SEABROOK.

   TOTAL....3 Officers, 7 N.C.Os and 38 men.

5. ASSEMBLY POINT.

   The whole raiding party will assemble in dugouts in the CHEMIN CREUX at - 30 minutes. The party will leave in the order laid down in paragraph 7 for the jumping-off point, moving by AVENUE "G" and Sap 21. They will be counted out by the O.C. Raiding Party.

6. JUMPING OFF POINT.

   The Jumping-off point will be to the right of and at the head of Sap 21. The party will be counted out here by 2/Lt. H.G.B. Sayers.

7. ADVANCE AND ASSAULT.

   At Zero entire raiding party will advance in the following order:-

   Blanket Party and Orderlies.
   Right and Left Blocking Parties.
   Right and Left Raiding Parties.
   Rear Party.

   The Blanket party must reach the wire slightly in advance of the Right and Left Blocking parties. The two Blanket men will throw their blankets on to the wire and withdraw to the sides, 2/Lt. SEABROOK, his two Orderlies and the raiding party, less rear party, passing over. If the blankets are not required the Blanket men will pass through the gap and remain as Orderlies, with 2/Lt. SEABROOK.
   2/Lt. SEABROOK will establish his report centre at the point of entry. He will remain there throughout the raid, and will be responsible for the passing back of prisoners, wounded etc., and for the improvement of the passage through the wire. (This is to be done by the blanket men). At the recall Signall he will count out the two raiding parties. The O.C. of each raiding party will report to him as they leave the trench.

When all are out he will withdraw on the rear party, bringing them in with him and covering the retirement of the raiding parties. In case of emergency he will be responsible for utilising the rear party to the best advantage. The N.C.O. will assist him in his duties. The two Orderlies will, during the advance, each lay a thick trail of paper from sandbags which they will carry.

The right and left blocking parties will closely follow the blanket party, being led by their respective Officers they will immediately follow 2/Lt. SEABROOK through or over the wire and leap into the trenches at the point reached by him. Right party to the right and left party to the left. They will be seen into the trench by their respective Officers. The Right blocking party will proceed down the German trench, to The Right blocking party trench junction at A.23.d.95.83. where they will form a block. Any prisoners taken by the blocking parties will be immediately passed back to their raiding parties. These blocking parties must get to their objectives with as little delay as possible, it is not their duty to bomb dugouts, etc., en route. Immediately behind the blocking parties will move the raiding parties led by their N.C.O.'s They will enter the trench at the same point as the blocking parties, and headed by their Officers will work down the trench right and left, cleaning it up, bombing dugouts, and doing all possible damage until either the Recall Signal is given or the bombing block is reached.

The rear party will follow raiding parties, the junior N.C.O. leading, the senior N.C.O. in rear. The senior N.C.O. will be responsible for dropping two men as connecting files each 20 yards, the last two being within easy range of the gap in the enemy's wire. This party will be responsible for keeping connecting between the raiding party and the Officer's post in Sap 21, for passing back prisoners and wounded, and for covering the retirement of the raiding party. In case of emergency they will they will act under 2/Lt. SEABROOK's oreers. The N.C.O.'s in charge, however, will take immediate action on their own initiative in case of any flanking move on the party of the enemy. They will report any action which they have taken immediately to the Officer's post in Sap 21 after the raid.

8. RECALL.

At plus 15 minutes Officers and N.C.O.s in charge of blocking and raiding parties will withdraw their respective parties leaving by the point of entry and reporting to 2nd Lieut. SEABROOK en route. Officers will be the last of their parties to leave the trench. Blocking parties will cover the retirement of the raiding parties to the point of exit. They will make their way as rapidly as possible to the jumping-off point (head of Sap 21) being directed by the connecting files of the rear party. On reaching this point they will be counted in by the Officer posted there, and moved down the sap to the BONNAL, thence via AVENUE "G" to the assembly dugougs in CHEMIN CREUX, where the final count will be made. When all the above are clear, 2nd Lieut. SEABROOK will withdraw the blanket and rear parties in the manner laid down in para 7. via the same routes as above. These parties being also counted in, in same manner as above.
Signal of Recall:- Rat-a-tat-tat from Machine Guns.

9. ARTILLERY.
    (a) The XVII Corps Heavy Howitzers intend carrying out counter-battery work commencing at - 2 minutes.
    (b) O.C. Right Group will co-operate as under:-
        (i) Feiht bombardment from plus 2 to plus 2.20 minutes. Bombardment on German front line on each side of point A.23.a.00.35.
From plus 2.20 to plus 2.40 minutes box barrage on German lines in rear and on each side of point A.23.a.00.35.

The above will be carried out by Field Guns.
(ii) From plus 10 minutes to "Cease Fire" bombardment of Trench junctions A.23.b.50.20. A.23.b.00.50, A.23.a. 55.90, and selected T.M. Emplacements by 4.5-howitzers and 2" T.Ms.

10. STOKES GUNS.
    (a) From - 4 hours to -3.50 hours dummy bombardment on German front line between points A.23.c.98.98 and A.23.d. 05.83 by 4 guns. 600 rounds.

    (b) From plus 10 to plus 15 minutes bombardment of German trench junctions between A.23.a.00.35 and A.23.a.40.40 by 4 guns. 300 rounds.

    Dugouts for teams will be provided for in the BONNAL trench. The O.C. 181 T.M. Battery to arrange to deal with any emergency that may arise.

11. LEWIS GUNS.
    Lieut. L.J. Oppenheimer will arrange that both flanks of the raiding party are protected by Lewis Gun fire in case of need.

12. The O.C. 181 Machine Gun Company will co-operate by bursts of fire from zero to plus 10 minutes on usual trench junctions. From plus 10 minutes to plus 15 minutes he will cease fire. From plus 15 minutes to cease-fire he will fire his rat-antat-tat, which will act as "Recall Signal".

13. Major A.G. PEMBERTON, O.C. "A" Company will make all necessary arrangements for dealing with any serious counter offensive on the part of the enemy.

14. The remainder of the Battalion and "D" Company, 2/21st L.R. at ABRI CENTRALE will stand to in their dugouts with a sentry posted over each.

15. COMMUNICATIONS.
    An advanced telephone station will be installed at the head of Sap 21. Here 2/Lt. SAYERS will be stationed and will be responsible for the reporting of progress of "A" Coy.H.Q. who will transmit it to B.H.Q. Two runners will be attached to him there. It is an absolute necessity that information, even of a negative character, should be forwarded to B.H.Q. every 3 minutes. 2/Lt. SAYERS will, in addition, be responsible for both the counting out and in of the entire raiding party. Os.C. Companies are responsible that no messages except those of a tactical nature are sent over the telephone from - 30 minutes to the receipt of the "Normal conditions" message.

16. CONTROL POSTS.
    A control post will be established by O.C. "A" Coy. in the BONNAL 40 yds. either side of the junction of Sap 21, and no traffic will be allowed between these points from -30 minutes to "Normal conditions". Between the above times, there will be no movement in the trenches except of men on special duty, and all down traffic will give way to up traffic.

17. An ADVANCED DRESSING STATION will be established in the BONNAL. All necessary arrangements as to extra personnel and stretchers to be made by the M.O. direct with the Advanced Dressing Station, ANZIN.

18. DRESS.
    All men of the raid party, except blanket men, will wear steel helmets and Service Dress with puttees, but will not wear equipment. All articles and marks on clothing that might

lead to identification will be removed and no personal letters or effects to be carried. Lieut. BAKER will be responsible for this. Special identity discs will be issued to each Officer and man. Faces will be blackened, and empty bandoliers worn round the chest passing over the right shoulder, and white tape round both shoulder straps.

19. ARMS, etc., CARRIED BY "RAIDING" PARTY.

Each N.C.O. and man who carries a rifle will have a round in the chamber, 4 in the magazine and 10 rounds in the right hand side pocket of his tunic.

2/Lt. SEABROOK..........Rifle and Fixed Bayonet.

Blanket Party.
- N.C.O..................Rifle & Fixed Bayonet & Wire cutters.
- 2 Blanket men..........Slung rifle, belt with bayonet, wire blanket, wire cutters.
- 2 Orderlies............Rifle & Bayonet, wire cutters, sandbags filled with paper.

Right & Left Blocking parties.
- N.C.Os.................Rifle & fixed bayonet, two bombs in left side pocket.
- 2 Bayonet men..........   -do-
- 1 Bomber..............Life preserver, bucket of 10 bombs.
- 2 Carriers............Life preserver, bucket of 10 bombs.

Raiding parties.
- Officers..............Revolver, two bombs in left side pocket.
- N.C.Os................Revolver, two bombs in left side pocket, one Very Pistol each, one cartridge in breech 3 in right breast pocket.
- Other Ranks..........Rifle & bayonet, two bombs in left side pocket.

Rear Party.............Rifle and Bayonet, 20 rounds in right hand side pocket.

20. Watches of all concerned will be synchronised at B.H.Q. at 5 p.m. the afternoon before the raid is to take place.

21. PRISONERS.

Men will be detailed from each raiding party whose duty it will be to take any prisoners captured to 2/Lt. SEABROOK who will pass them back to BONNAL via Sap 21, whence they will be brought direct to B.H.Q. O.C. "A" Coy. will provide necessary escorts. Route via AVENUE "G" and COLLECTEUR.

22. The code "MESSAGE RECEIVED" will be issued from Bn. H.Q. when normal conditions may be resumed.

23. All ranks must understand the absolute necessity of pushing straight through to their objective without being diverted by any flanking bombing attack or rifle fire.

24. Silence must be maintained throughout the entire operation.

25. All ranks will be warned that, in the event of their being captured by the enemy, they will on no account give the name of their regiment, Brigade or Division, but state their number name and initials only.

26. A hot meal will be served to the raiding party on return.

27. ACKNOWLEDGE.

14/10/16.

Major.
Cmdg. 2/23rd Bn. The London Regt.

Report of Raid made by the

2/23rd Battalion The London Regt

on night of 14/15th October 1916 on enemy's lines.

The scheme as laid down in orders issued by me was rigidly adhered to. At - 4 hours on the 14/10/16, 6 Stokes Guns opened fire on that part of the enemy's lines which it was intended to raid. The fire from these guns was very accurate, and did considerable damage to the enemy's front line. In all, 650 rounds were fired. The result of this was retaliation of a very heavy nature, which lasted for about one hour. During this period the enemy threw over all classes of shells and Trench Mortars. Up to this time we suffered no casualties.

The Heavy artillery opened punctually at - 2 minutes on counter battery work.

The Right Group opened a feint bombardment from plus 2 to plus 2.20 minutes, bombarding the enemy's front on each side of A.23.a.00.35. From plus 2.20 to plus 2.40 mins. the artillery opened a feint box barrage at the same point. The firing of these guns was most effective, and was well directed. 4 Stokes Guns also co-operated in this feint bombardment from plus 4 minutes, firing in all about 450 shells. There is no doubt that this feint bombardment had the effect of drawing, at that time, the whole of the enemy retaliation, as the sector opposite was subjected to fire of every description.

While this was in progress our raiding party, which left the jumping off point at minus 2 minutes, were successfully enabled to cross No man's land without casualties. The Raiding party carried out the programme exactly, proceeding across no man's land in perfect order. The wire was found to be well cut, and was easily negotiated with the aid of the blankets. Upon 2/Lt SEABROOK, who was leading the party, reaching the German Trench he was met by 2 sentries, at whom he fired. They immediately ran away. The whole party as arranged entered the trench, dispersing to the right and left. The Left blocking party proceeded down the trench followed by the Left Raiding Party under Lieut. Baker, for a distance of about 60 yards. This party did not encounter or see any Germans. They however bombed one dug-out on the parapet side. All of the left party returned. The party going to the right preceded by the bombing block encountered one German who was shot dead. This man's cap and rifle were brought back. The Blocking party proceeded about 40 or 50 yards where they came to a communication trench and established a block. This party on their way were bombed and shot at from a dug-out. The raiding party called down the dug-out for the occupants to come out but they received no reply, and therefore bombed the dugout. The next dugout was also bombed. On the return journey this party encountered no opposition, but Germans were closely following the Blocking Party, throwing bombs at them all the way. I regret to say that during this return journey of the Blocking Party one bomber was killed, one had his leg blown to pieces, and another one was injured. This party now consisted of above three ~~sixfour~~ and ~~included~~ one unwounded Corporal. Every effort was made by the two latter to bring back the dead man and the severely wounded man, but without avail, the unwounded Corporal having eventually to bring in the third man (wounded). These two left the trench before arriving at the point of entry, and had to creep

- 2 -

through the German wire, hence their delay in arriving back. Mr. SEABROOK, the Officer at the point of entry, was the last to leave his point, and was attacked by several Germans while he was awaiting the last of the party. After a fight, during which he bayonetted one, he was compelled to leave.

The total number of casualties are as follows:-

1 Officer slightly wounded
1 man missing, believed killed.
1 man missing and severely wounded.
7 men wounded.

Of the above 7, one was wounded in the German Trench, and the remaining 6 sustained their injuries through enemy barbed wire and shrapnel on the return journey through no man's land.

The information received with regard to the condition of the German Trenches was that they were very wide, and very badly knocked about. With the exception of there being a few dugouts and trench boards, one would hardly have known they were trenches.

The following booty was brought back:-

1 Cap (which has been sent to Headquarters)
2 rifles.

I have made most careful enquiries, and it is satisfactory to note that the duties allotted to the several members of this raiding party were all carried out exactly as laid down.

Victor F. Seyd
Major
Commanding 2/23rd Battalion The London Regt.

15/10/16.

1916

War Diary

2/23 London. R.

For

November, 1916.

Army Form C. 2118

WAR DIARY
or
INTELLIGENCE SUMMARY 2/23 Batt. London Regt.
(Erase heading not required.)

Instructions regarding War Diaries and Intelligence Summaries are contained in F.S. Regs., Part II. and the Staff Manual respectively. Title Pages will be prepared in manuscript.

Place	Date	Hour	Summary of Events and Information	Remarks and references to Appendices
CANDAS	Nov 1st	Weather. FINE early. HEAVY SHOWERS during aft.	General training, demonstrations by Divisional Gas N.C.O's as to mode of wearing small Box Respirators. 4-30 P.M. Inspection of Battalion by Lieut. Sir Douglas Haig. G.C.B, G.C.V.O, K.C.I.E, A.D.C. Commander-in-Chief, British Armies in France.	a.s.C.
"	2nd	WET morning FINE later	General training indoors during forenoon. Route marching, digging &c during afternoon. Practice alarm - orders received & issued to Coy. at 6.41 PM Battalion ready to move off at 6.41 PM	a.s.C.
"	3rd	FINE	General training, extensive digging &c.	a.s.C.
"	4th	WET early FINE midday WET evening.	Battalion moved by march route from CANDAS to ERGNIES & billetted.	a.s.C.
ERGNIES	5th	FINE	Church Parade. Interior economy & Rifle inspection, general cleaning up.	a.s.C.

1875 W. W593/826 1,000,000 4/15 J.B.C. & A. A.D.S.S./Forms/C.2118.

Army Form C. 2118

WAR DIARY
or
INTELLIGENCE SUMMARY
(Erase heading not required.)

2/23 London Regt.

Place	Date	Hour	Summary of Events and Information	Remarks and references to Appendices
ERGNIES	Nov. 6	Weather. Showery	Physical Training, Route Marches &c. 2 Lt MATTHEWS proceeded to 5th Army School being under age.	A.S.C.
"	7	WET	Bathing Parades, Physical Training &c.	A.S.C.
"	8	HEAVY SHOWERY	General Training. 6 Officers & 9 Ranks proceeded on leave.	A.S.C.
"	9	FINE	General Training, Practice Attack, Physical Training, Route Marches &c.	A.S.C.
"	10	SHOWERY	General Training, Practice Attack, Physical Training &c. 4 Officers & 7 Ranks proceeded on leave	A.S.C.
"	11	WET	General Training &c. 20 men found unfit by Medical Board sent to Base.	A.S.C.
"	12	FINE	Church Parade. Lantomer Economy & inspection of Billets by C.O. Draft of 14 men arrived from Base.	A.S.C.

WAR DIARY or INTELLIGENCE SUMMARY

2/23 London Regt.

Army Form C. 2118

(Erase heading not required.)

Place	Date	Hour	Summary of Events and Information	Remarks and references to Appendices
ERQUINGHEM	Nov. 13	Fine to Misty.	General Training &c. Draft of 13 men arrived from Base. 2 Officers & 2 O.Ranks proceeded on leave.	A.S.C.
"	14	Fine	General Training &c.	A.S.C.
"	15	Fine	General Training &c. 3. R.A.M.C. men reported for Water duty.	A.S.C.
"	16	Fine & Cold	General Training. Battalion practice in the attack. Blankets & clothing of Battalion disinfected.	A.S.C.
"	17	Fine & Cold.	General Training &c. Capt. Owen returned to duty.	A.S.C.
"	18	Showery.	General Training. &c. 2.Lts. G.B. Lewis & H.J. Potts reported for duty. Lt. Nix (R.A.M.C) reported for duty as Medical Officer, vice Capt. Bell, sick admitted Hospital in England whilst on leave.	A.S.C.

Army Form C. 2118

WAR DIARY
or
INTELLIGENCE SUMMARY

2/23 Batt. London Regt

(Erase heading not required.)

Instructions regarding War Diaries and Intelligence Summaries are contained in F.S. Regs., Part II. and the Staff Manual respectively. Title Pages will be prepared in manuscript.

Place	Date	Hour	Summary of Events and Information	Remarks and references to Appendices
	Mar.	Weather		
ERGNIES	19th	Dull	Church Parade. Inspection of Billets by Major SEYD.	
"	20	Dull & Cold	General Training. Route March &c. Capt BELL (RAMC) on duty & 2nd Lt Hix not to Field Ambulance.	W.N.C.
"	21	FINE	General Training	W.N.C.
"	22	FINE	Cleaning up & preparing to move. Lt HEPWORTH & 2nd Lt McNULLOP 2/24 L. Reg. — 2nd Lt BEENEY 2/22 — 2nd Lt WALL 2/6 reported for duty on transfer. 7. Mantoes 2/21 1st Regt & 2. O. Rantoes 2/22 L.R. reported for duty.	W.N.C.
"	23	FINE	Reveille 3 AM. Battalion moved by march route @ 5/10 AM to LONGPRE Sg. & entrained en-route for MARSEILLES leaving station at 12-55 PM & shunted to siding finally moving off at 1-40 PM. Capt OWEN, 2nd Lt MATTHEWS & 2nd Lt TURNER left behind & struck off strength. 7 N.C.O's approved for Commissions & 6 men found unfit left behind & struck off strength.	W.N.C.

1875 W.: W593/826 1,000,000 4/15 J.B.C. & A. A.D.S.S./Forms/C. 2118.

Army Form C. 2118

WAR DIARY
or
INTELLIGENCE SUMMARY
(Erase heading not required.)

2/23. Batt. London Regt.

Instructions regarding War Diaries and Intelligence Summaries are contained in F.S. Regs., Part II. and the Staff Manual respectively. Title Pages will be prepared in manuscript.

Place	Date	Hour	Summary of Events and Information	Remarks and references to Appendices
ENROUTE for MARSEILLES	Nov 24	FINE Weather	Train arrived at MONTREAU & halted for 1 hour, train stopped at DIJON @ 4 PM for about 10 minutes, arrived MACON @ 10 PM stopped 50 minutes	are
"	25	FINE	Train arrived PIERRELATTE @ 9-25 AM left @ 10-25 AM and arrived at MARSEILLES at 5 P.M. and marched to Camp CARCASSONNE and billetted under canvas	are
"	26	FINE	General cleaning up &c. Draft of 76. O. Ranks arrived.	are
"	27	FINE	General Training	are
"	28	FINE	General Training & Short route march	are
"	29	FINE	General Training & Short route march	are
"	30	FINE	General Training & Short route march	are

Crawbull
Lieut Col
Commanding 2/23 London Regt.

www.ingramcontent.com/pod-product-compliance
Lightning Source LLC
Chambersburg PA
CBHW081450160426
43193CB00013B/2436